AN
EDWARDIAN CHRISTMAS

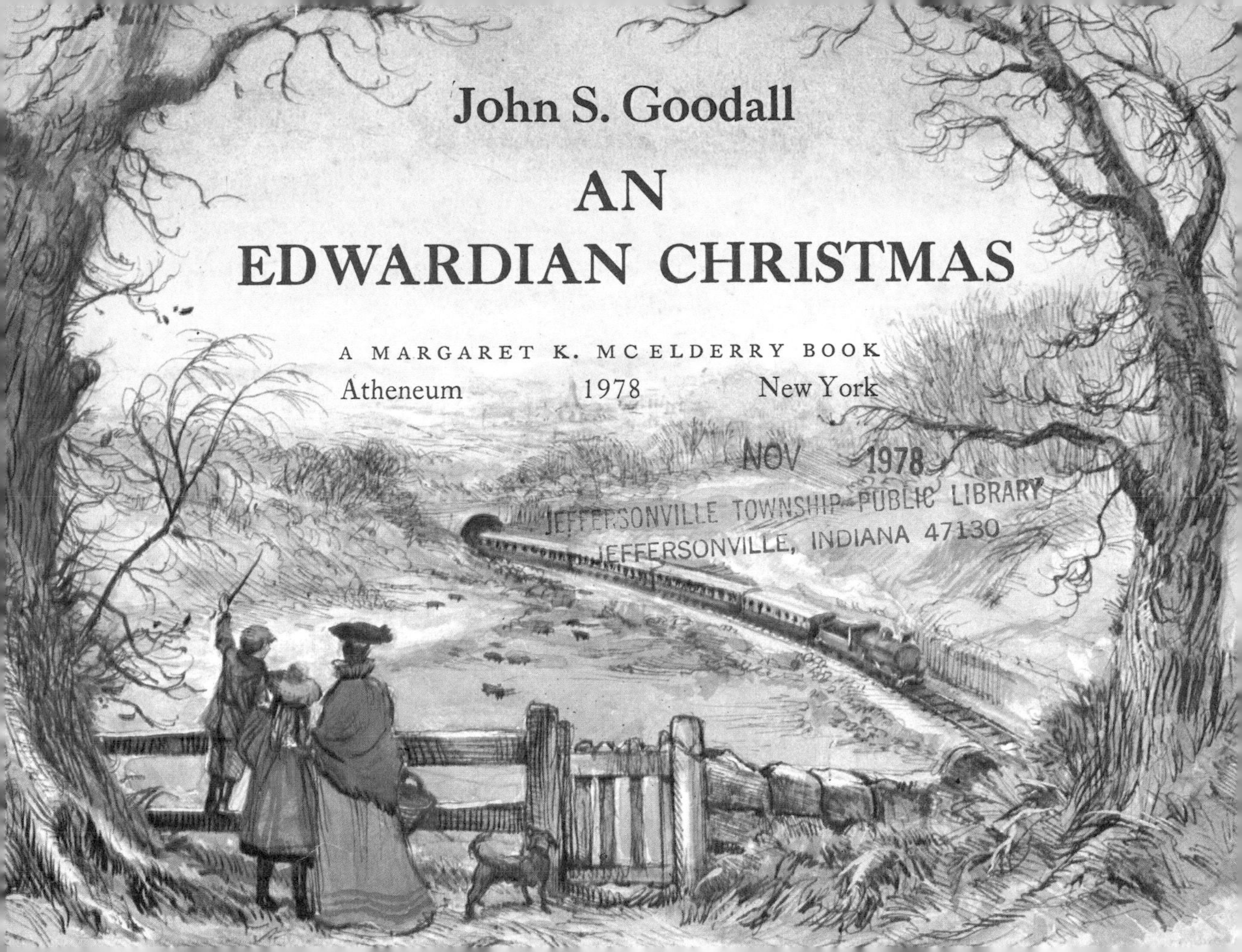

John S. Goodall

AN EDWARDIAN CHRISTMAS

A MARGARET K. MCELDERRY BOOK
Atheneum 1978 New York

j-e

G64le2ec

Library of Congress catalog card number 77-4580
ISBN 0-689-50106-4
Printed in Great Britain
First American Edition 1978

For Margaret,
Sarah and Lavinia,
With Love

Pears' Soap
EXIT
NOTICE
B

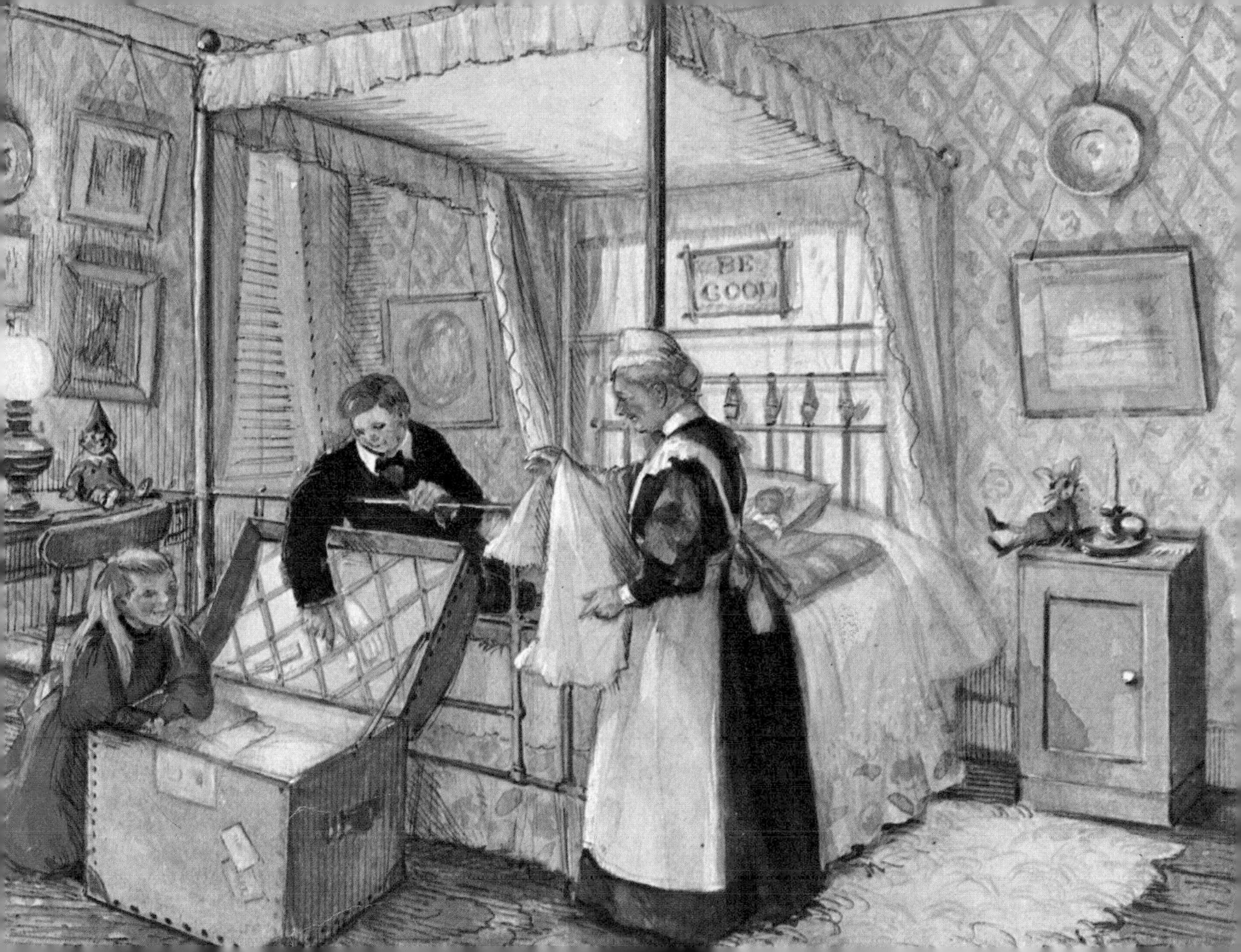
BE GOOD

J. BROWN. FAMILY BUTCHERS
TRY OUR NOTED SAUSAGES
WELSH MEAT

G. SMITH.
PROVISION STORES
HAPPY XMA
OXO

FOX & HOUNDS INN

GOD IS LOVE

BARGAINS
Half Price

GREAT REDUCTIONS
WINTER SALE
BARGAINS

B. POLLOCK
Publishers